ACHIEVE LEVEL 3

Writing

BY RICHARD COOPER
AND SHIRLEY ARMER

RISING STARS

Rising Stars UK Ltd., 76 Farnaby Road, Bromley, BR1 4BH
Website: www.risingstars-uk.com

Every effort has been made to trace copyright holders and obtain their permission for the use of copyright material. The authors and publishers will gladly receive information enabling them to rectify any error or omission in subsequent editions.

All facts are correct at time of going to press.

New Edition 2003
Published 2003
First published 2002
Text, design and layout © Rising Stars UK Ltd.

Editorial: Tanya Solomons
Design: Starfish Design for Print
Illustrations: copyright © Burville-Riley
Cover photo: copyright © Getty Images

Rising Stars are grateful to Jane Bovey of Warren Road Primary School for her help and advice on this new edition.

All rights reserved. No part of this publication may be reproduced, stored in a retrieval system, or transmitted, in any form by any means, electronic, mechanical, photocopying, recording or otherwise, without the prior permission of Rising Stars UK Ltd.

British Library Cataloguing in Publication Data
A CIP record for this book is available from the British Library.

ISBN 1-904591-29-9

Printed at Wyndham Gait, Grimsby, UK

Contents

How to use this book 4

LEVEL 2 – THE TRICKY BITS
Grammar 6
Vocabulary 8
Handwriting 10
Syllables 11
Speech marks 12

LEVEL 3
Spelling 14
Grammar 2 18
Planning and writing a story 20
Story endings 22
Writing a story 23
Writing a book review 24
Writing instructions 26
Writing a recount 28
Writing letters 30
Information writing 32
Punctuation 34
Using conjunctions 36
Using time connectives 38
Vocabulary choices 40

KEY FACTS
The Key Stage 1 Tests 42
Helping your child do well 44

ANSWERS 46

How to use this book

1. **Introduction section** – This section tells you what your child needs to do to get a Level 3. It picks out what the key learning objective is and explains it simply.

2. **The question** – The question helps your child to 'learn by doing'. It is presented in a similar way to the SATs questions and gives you a real example to work with.

3. **The flow chart** – This shows the steps to use when completing questions like this. Some of the advice happens on every flow chart (Read the question then read it again).

4. **The Star Tips** – How to get to grips with each topic.

5. **The Star characters** – They explain the concepts being covered and offer support and an encouraging word at the right time.

6. **Practice questions** – This is where the children have to do the work! Try each question using the technique explained in the flow chart and then check the answers at the back.

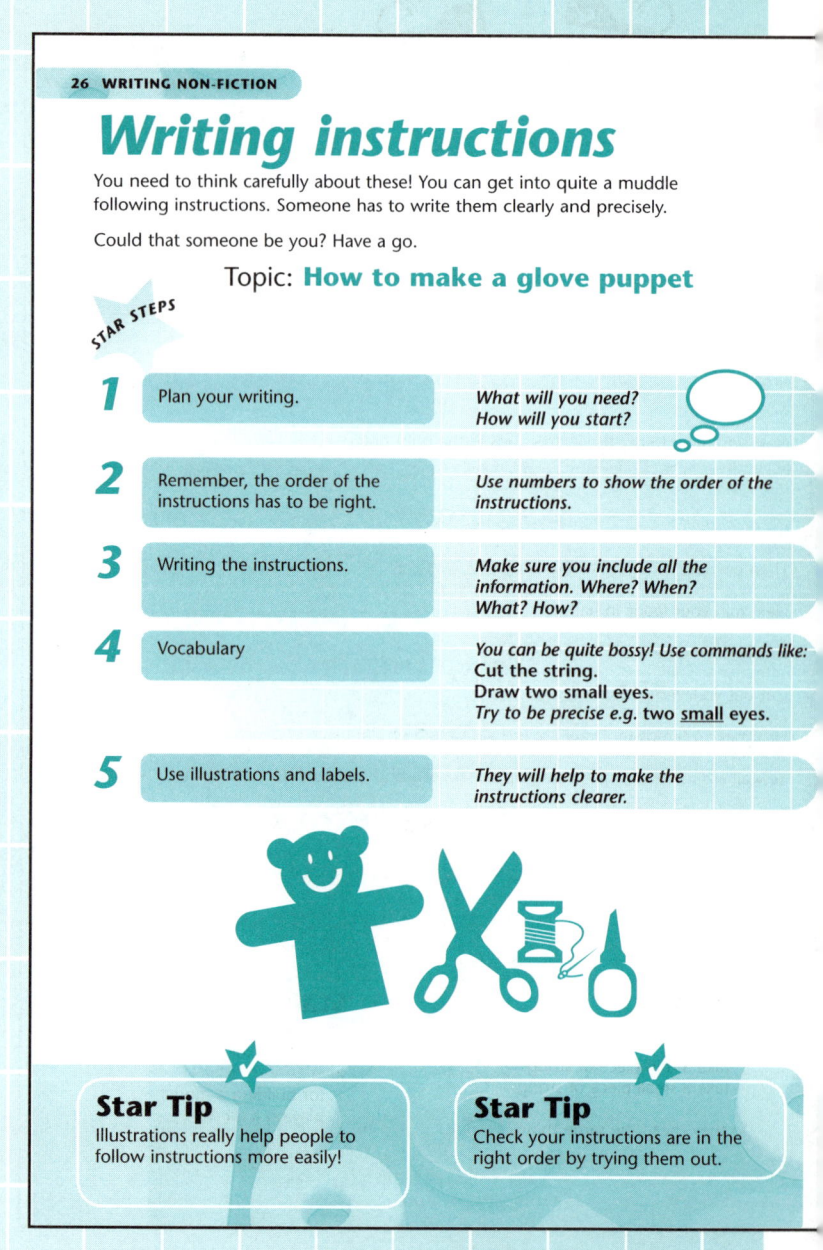

---

26 WRITING NON-FICTION

Writing instructions

You need to think carefully about these! You can get into quite a muddle following instructions. Someone has to write them clearly and precisely.

Could that someone be you? Have a go.

Topic: How to make a glove puppet

STAR STEPS

1. Plan your writing. — What will you need? How will you start?

2. Remember, the order of the instructions has to be right. — Use numbers to show the order of the instructions.

3. Writing the instructions. — Make sure you include all the information. Where? When? What? How?

4. Vocabulary — You can be quite bossy! Use commands like: Cut the string. Draw two small eyes. Try to be precise e.g. two small eyes.

5. Use illustrations and labels. — They will help to make the instructions clearer.

Star Tip
Illustrations really help people to follow instructions more easily!

Star Tip
Check your instructions are in the right order by trying them out.

WRITING NON-FICTION 27

Making a glove puppet

Help to finish the instructions by drawing the illustrations.

You will need:

pencil ☐ scissors ☐ fabric ☐ pins ☐

thread ☐ needle ☐ felt pens ☐ paper ☐

Now you need to get the instructions in the right order!

Order these muddled instructions by putting numbers in the boxes.

Then pin your template to the fabric. ☐

Next fold your fabric in half. ☐

Finally draw on a face. ☐

Cut out your template. ☐

First make a template. Draw around your hand on the piece of paper. [1]

Sew all around the edge of the puppet, sewing both pieces of fabric together. ☐

Cut around the template through both layers of fabric. ☐

Did you spot the clues we gave you? Words like *first*, *then*, and *next* help to get things in the right order!

Star Tip
Choose describing words carefully.
- Take a thin piece of string.
- Take a small piece of string.

Do they mean the same thing?

Star Tip
You need to be able to follow instructions for lots of things, such as:
★ for building a model
★ playing a game
★ recipes
★ operating a video

How to use the book with your child:

1. Focus on ONE topic each time. Read through the introduction and the question.

2. Follow the flow chart through (make notes if it helps your child).

3. Try some practice questions.

4. Check your answers and look again at the Star Tips and flow chart.

What we have included:

We have put in those topics at Level 1 and 2 that children often find difficult. These are at the front of the book and give a more gentle introduction to the material. They are presented in a similar way to the Level 3 content, so doing this section first will help children to become accustomed to the style of the book.

We have also included all the content that children will need for a Level 3.

We have also included all the answers to the practice questions!

GOOD LUCK!

Grammar

Grammar helps your writing make sense.

★ Remember to check your work!

★ Make sure your sentences are in the right order!

Check this sentence.

Leo up ran to the park.

Can you see which words need to change?

Answer: **Leo *ran up* to the park.**

Practice questions

Put these sentences in the right order.

1 Gemma put hat her on.
   _____

2 Robert in went to the shop.
   _____

3 The dog brown was barking.
   _____

4 Cats like to sleep in sun the.
   _____

Star Tip
Always re-read your writing to check for silly mistakes.

Star Tip
Look at the pages on punctuation too.

LEVEL 2 – THE TRICKY BITS   7

Another important way to make sure your sentences make sense is to check the tense. No, not tents, **tense**!

Past tense
Something that happened before.

I watched the fireworks last night.

Present tense
Something that is happening now.

I am eating my ice cream.

Future tense
Something that is going to happen.

I will take the bus to school tomorrow.

Practice questions

Try writing the past, present and future tenses of these phrases.

past	present	future
1 I rode	I _____	I will ride
2 I sang	I am singing	I _____
3 We _____	We are writing	We will write

See if you can spot the mistakes in these sentences.

1 She write her letter yesterday. (_____)

2 I will played at school today. (_____)

3 Marie swim ten lengths of the pool. (_____)

4 Jack will drove to school tomorrow. (_____)

Star Tip
Do you sentences begin with a capital letter and end with a full stop?

LEVEL 2 – THE TRICKY BITS

Vocabulary

Another way to make your writing more interesting is to use **adjectives**. Adjectives are describing words. They help the reader **see** your ideas in their mind.

Question: How can we turn this sentence into a brilliant description?

STAR STEPS

The dog barked at me.

1	Read the question then read it again.	*Read the sentence carefully.*
2	Read the sentence aloud.	*This helps you hear ideas.*
3	Think of adjectives you could use.	huge, brown, scary, vicious, wild, cute, horrible
4	Choose a word that describes the dog.	The cute dog barked at me. ✗
5	Does your sentence make sense? If not, choose another adjective.	The vicious dog barked at me. ✓

Practice questions

Add adjectives to these words to make them sound really exciting!

1 _____ witch   2 _____ tiger   3 _____ stars

4 _____ apples   5 _____ king   6 _____ monsters

LEVEL 2 – THE TRICKY BITS

You can also add to your writing by using **adverbs**. Adverbs are describing words too. They describe verbs. Lots of adverbs end in 'ly'.

Question: **How can we make the verb in this sentence really stand out?**

STAR STEPS

Ramon walked towards the dark tunnel.

1 Read the question then read it again. — *Read the sentence carefully.*

2 Read the sentence aloud. — *Listen to the ideas as you read.*

3 Think of adverbs you could use. — **quickly, sadly, slowly, happily, worriedly, luckily**

4 Choose a word that describes *how* Ramon walked. — **Ramon walked luckily towards the dark tunnel.** ✗

5 Does your sentence make sense? If not, choose another adverb. — **Ramon walked slowly towards the dark tunnel.** ✓

Practice questions

Add adverbs to these verbs to make them sound more exciting.

1 ran _____   2 smiled _____   3 cried _____

4 chewed _____   5 worked _____   6 drove _____

These words might help you get started:
noisily, cleverly, quickly, happily, slowly, miserably

LEVEL 2 – THE TRICKY BITS

Handwriting

If you want to have neat handwriting, you need to:
- ★ keep practising
- ★ keep your letters the same size
- ★ show tall letters and tails clearly

Practise getting these letters all the same size.

c o a

r n m

e i s

v w x

Now practise showing tall letters and tails clearly.

a l t

c b d

e h k

f g j

p q y

Syllables

Syllables are parts of words. They contain a single vowel sound.

These are words with one syllable.

cat   **dog**   **star**   **fish**   **hand**

These are words with two syllables.

happy	**tiger**	**brother**	**started**
ha-pee	tie-ger	bru-ther	star-ted

These are words with three syllables.

telephone   **Saturday**   **another**
tel-e-fone   Sat-er-day   a-nu-ther

How many syllables do each of these names have? Say them out loud and write the number of syllables in the box next to each name.

Joshua ☐   Una ☐   Rebecca ☐   Kevin ☐

Keith ☐   Bethany ☐   Laura ☐

Robert ☐   Francis ☐

Star Tip
When you are spelling difficult words, try to hear each syllable in the word.

Star Tip
Try to **feel** the syllables. Put your hand on your chin. As you say a word your chin drops for each new syllable.

Speech marks

"I've told you before. You need speech marks around the words characters actually say in your stories," yelled Mrs Cranky, our teacher.

This is called direct speech. It means someone in your story is talking. You need to put speech marks like this " at the start of their speech and like this " when they have finished.

Practice questions

Try putting speech marks into these sentences.

1   Well done to you all, said Mrs Cranky.

2   Try throwing underarm Jack, advised his mum.

3   I don't care! yelled the strange girl.

4   Please take us to the pictures, we begged.

5   Mum called up the stairs to us, Have you tidied your room?

6   Do you know the park is closed asked the park keeper?

7   Tom shouted again I'm not going with you!

8   Your project must be finished by tomorrow! the teacher bellowed.

9   Why do you have to be so noisy? moaned Gran.

10 I hope you like it, Dad beamed.

Star Tip
Speech marks go at the beginning **and** the end of each bit of speech.

LEVEL 2 – THE TRICKY BITS 13

How did they say that?
It is important to vary your direct speech so that characters say things in exciting ways.
   "I want a sweet!" said Amanda is a good sentence

but "I want a sweet!" demanded Amanda is better.

Practice questions

Re-write these sentences using a more exciting word than 'said'. Don't forget to put in the speech marks!

1 "Wash the dishes," said Mum.
   _____

2 "Come and see the flowers," said Annie.
   _____

3 "Watch out!" we said to the others.
   _____

4 "I slipped in the mud," said Frank.
   _____

5 "I have lost my ball," said Jack
   _____

6 "Please take us to the park, Auntie Suzy," we said.
   _____

7 "Ow! My arm stings!" said Harry.
   _____

Star Tip
You can say 'said' in many ways. Here are some examples: *demanded, shouted, screamed, whispered, ordered, called, told, laughed, sighed, pleaded, whined.*

SPELLING

Spelling

Now it's time for some spelling training!
Spelling superstars need to keep fit and this is how they do it.

Look   Say   Cover   Write   Check

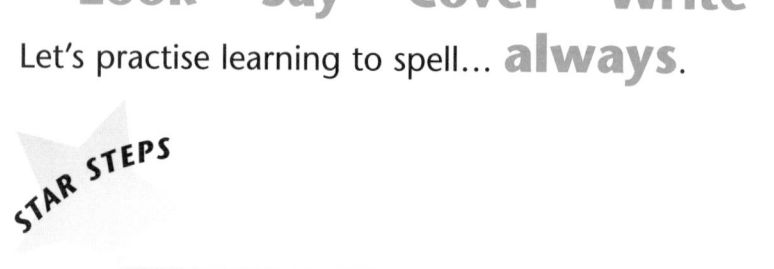

Let's practise learning to spell… **always**.

STAR STEPS

1 Look — Notice the shape of the word. Always look for tall letters and letters with tails.

2 Say — Say the whole word. Then say each letter: a, l, w, a, y, s

3 Cover — Cover the word and spell it aloud.

4 Write — Write the word as you say it aloud again.

5 Check — Check your spelling.

Star Tip

Try saying a word exactly as it is written, not as it usually sounds.

Wed nes day
Feb ru ary
diff er ent

Star Tip

Look for words hidden inside other words.

often 'ten'
hear   'ear'
notice 'ice'

SPELLING 15

Practise these words – they are grouped in spelling patterns to help you.
Remember:

Look Say Cover Write Check

able	_____	helpful	_____
table	_____	careful	_____
single	_____	useful	_____
bottle	_____	wonderful	_____

some	_____	also	_____
something	_____	almost	_____
sometimes	_____	always	_____
somewhere	_____	although	_____

follow	_____	come	_____
hollow	_____	become	_____
pillow	_____	welcome	_____
below	_____	coming	_____

other	_____	never	_____
another	_____	number	_____
mother	_____	father	_____
brother	_____	under	_____

Why do elephants all have grey trunks? Because they belong to the same swimming club!

Star Tip
Make up your own rhyme or story to help you remember tricky words, like 'because'.

Big
Elephants
Can
Always
Understand
Small
Elephants

SPELLING

More spelling practice

Here are some useful words. Make sure you know them.

Remember:

Look Say Cover Write Check

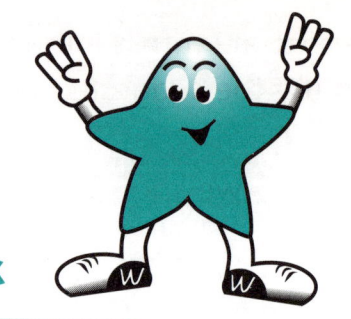

Monday _____	Friday _____
Tuesday _____	Saturday _____
Wednesday _____	Sunday _____
Thursday _____	Today _____

January _____	July _____
February _____	August _____
March _____	September _____
April _____	October _____
May _____	November _____
June _____	December _____

red _____	orange _____
yellow _____	green _____
blue _____	indigo _____
violet _____	pink _____
purple _____	brown _____
black _____	white _____

one _____	six _____
two _____	seven _____
three _____	eight _____
four _____	nine _____
five _____	ten _____

Key words to learn

These words are the ones you need to know if you want to be a superstar speller.
Tick each word when you are SURE you know how to spell it.

☐ above	☐ don't	☐ morning	☐ think
☐ across	☐ during	☐ mother	☐ those
☐ almost	☐ earth	☐ much	☐ thought
☐ along	☐ every	☐ near	☐ through
☐ also	☐ eyes	☐ never	☐ today
☐ always	☐ father	☐ number	☐ together
☐ animals	☐ first	☐ often	☐ told
☐ any	☐ follow(ing)	☐ only	☐ tries
☐ around	☐ found	☐ opened	☐ turn(ed)
☐ asked	☐ friends	☐ other	☐ under
☐ baby	☐ garden	☐ outside	☐ until
☐ balloon	☐ goes	☐ own	☐ upon
☐ before	☐ gone	☐ paper	☐ used
☐ began	☐ great	☐ place	☐ walk(ed)(ing)
☐ being	☐ half	☐ right	☐ watch
☐ below	☐ happy	☐ round	☐ where
☐ better	☐ head	☐ second	☐ while
☐ between	☐ heard	☐ show	☐ white
☐ birthday	☐ high	☐ sister	☐ whole
☐ both	☐ I'm	☐ small	☐ why
☐ brother	☐ important	☐ something	☐ window
☐ brought	☐ inside	☐ sometimes	☐ without
☐ can't	☐ jumped	☐ sound	☐ woke(n)
☐ change	☐ knew	☐ started	☐ word
☐ children	☐ know	☐ still	☐ work
☐ clothes	☐ lady	☐ stopped	☐ world
☐ coming	☐ leave	☐ such	☐ write
☐ didn't	☐ light	☐ suddenly	☐ year
☐ different	☐ might	☐ sure	☐ young
☐ does	☐ money	☐ swimming	

Grammar 2
Structure of sentences

Simple sentences all contain a SUBJECT and a VERB.
They all start with a capital letter and end with a full stop.

Question: **Can you rearrange these words to make a proper sentence?**

STAR STEPS

shone The brightly. star

1	Read the question then read it again.	*I need to make these words make sense!*
2	Find the word with the capital letter.	*That's* **The**.
3	Which word makes sense after 'The'?	*The shone? …no!* *The brightly? …no!* *The star? …yes!*
4	Which is the next word that makes sense?	*The star brightly? …no!* *The star shone? …yes!*
5	The final word must have a full stop because it's the end of the sentence.	*The star shone brightly.* *There, I've done it.*
6	Which is the subject?	*Easy, the star.*
7	And the verb?	*Shone is the verb. It's the past tense of shine.*

Star Tip
Always read your sentences to see if they make sense.

Practice questions

Can you help Writing Star to rearrange these words into proper sentences?

1 poured   roof.   the   Rain   through

2 cats   milk.   like   Most

3 exploded   night   the   Fireworks   sky.   in

4 find   shells   lots   You   of   can   seashore.   the   on

Can you draw a line from the subject to the correct verb and ending? The first one has been done for you.

Subject	Verb and ending
The young boy	wagged excitedly.
A magic slipper	destroyed everything in its path.
My favourite toy	wished he could be like his older brother.
The startled horse	was just what he needed.
Leo's football boots	was on the Princess's foot.
The puppy's tail	is the bike I got for my birthday.
The raging hurricane	hurt his feet.
The relaxing holiday	bolted.

If you read these sentences WITHOUT the verb or subject, they don't make sense. Go on, try it out.

Star Tip
Double-check you have a capital letter at the beginning and a full stop at the end of each sentence.

Planning a story

Writing a good story can be great fun! It will help if you remember the five 'P's.

Previous Planning Prevents Poor Performance!

Follow this framework when you are planning a story and you will be on the way to becoming a great author.

What's an author?

Someone who writes books?

Story writing framework

Characters
Who is the main character?
Are the other characters good or bad, greedy or silly?

Star Tip
Don't write about your friends.
Make sure each character has a role.

Setting
Where and when will the story take place?
Is it in the 'real world' or in space or underground?

Star Tip
When: future, past, present?
Where: space, magical land, your school?

Beginning
What happens first? What is the problem that needs to be solved?

Star Tip
Start with an interesting sentence to get your reader interested.

WRITING FICTION 21

Middle
What happens next?
This is the exciting bit. How has the problem developed?

Star Tip
Get to the problem quickly. Don't spend ages getting to the big issues.

End
How will the story end?
This must relate back to the original problem. How was it solved? Is it believable?

Star Tip
Does it have a twist?

Other important parts of stories

Style
What type of story is this?
Is it a horror or adventure story? Is it a mystery or myth? How about a fairy tale?

Star Tip
Choose a style and stick to it through the whole story.

Vocabulary
What words or phrases could you use in the story to make it come alive?
What conjunctions or connectives can you use?
Are there any special words or names that you want in your story?

Star Tip
Make sure your words fit with your setting and style.

1st Person or 3rd Person
From whose point of view are your writing the story? Will it start:
First Person "I awoke with a start on a cold September morning…"
or
Third Person "Jamie awoke with a start on a cold September morning…"?

Star Tip
Choose one person and stick to it.

Story endings

Story endings are very tricky. Here are some key points to remember.

Do

- ★ Plan your story **and** the ending.
- ★ Make sure the ending makes sense.
- ★ Include all your characters in the ending.
- ★ Think about endings in books you read. They can give you ideas for your own stories.

Don't

Use these endings:

- ★ I had my tea and went to bed.
- ★ So we all went home.
- ★ It was just a dream.

Read these endings and decide which one is more interesting.

a We all said goodbye. I put the book back on the shelf and went home.

b We said our sad goodbyes. I would be sorry to leave this strange land and all my new friends but I knew they were safe with their new king. I was ready to go home and even ready to give my new school a chance. I closed my eyes. When I opened them, I was back in the dusty library. I put the book back on the shelf.

Explain why you think your choice is more interesting.

Star Tip
Happy endings work well because they make the reader feel good about your story.

Star Tip
A question at the end of your story can sound quite dramatic.
As I walked, I thought about my adventure. Who would be the next lucky person to pick up that incredible book?

Planning and writing a story

Choose a title (or use one of your own) and plan a story using the planning sheet. You could then write it at home or in school!

Titles

★ The Haunted Cellar
★ How the Crocodile got his Smile
★ The Search for Space Gold
★ The Three Little Ducks
★ The Mystery of Platform Nine

Title: _____

Beginning

Grab the reader's attention!

Middle

Build up the tension.

Ending

Tie up all the loose ends.

Writing a book review

Here's another type of writing for you to try.

STAR STEPS — You can pass on information to your friends about the books you read.

1 Plan your writing.

How will you start?
Did you like the story?
Did you like the pictures?
What were the characters like?

2 Remember to finish writing about one section before you move on to another.

Start a new paragraph for each section.

3 In a review the word to remember is **why**?

Why *are the pictures good?*
Why *did you like it?*
Why *is the wolf your favourite character?*

4 Vocabulary

Use these words in your writing:
author, illustrations, characters, beginning, ending

5 Show that you know someone will read your writing.

Use interesting words.
Tell them what you think.

Star Tip
Use interesting words, even if you're not sure how to spell them. Just have a go!

Star Tip
You could try to read book reviews in newspapers or magazines.

WRITING NON-FICTION 25

Planning your review

Think about a book you read recently and use the planning frame.
Then write out your review.

★ How will you start your writing?

Try these ideas:
If you like adventure stories, you will like this book.
or
The pictures in this book are very funny but you will enjoy the story as well.

_____
_____
_____

★ Did you like the story? Why?

Use words like
*enjoyable, funny, exciting, scary, interesting,
I liked, I thought,
because, although, however*

_____
_____
_____

★ Did you like the illustrations?

Use words like
style, realistic, cartoon, bright, frightening, detailed, colours

_____
_____
_____

★ What were the characters like?

Use lots of adjectives like
terrible, wicked, kind, beautiful, smart, tricky, mischievous, suspicious, helpful, interesting

_____
_____
_____

Star Tip
Remember, you can write about other things, such as the ending or other books the author has written.

Star Tip
Use adjectives to make your writing more interesting. You will find lots of adjectives in a thesaurus. See if you can find one at school or in a library.

Writing instructions

You need to think carefully about these! You can get into quite a muddle following instructions. Someone has to write them clearly and precisely.

Could that someone be you? Have a go.

Topic: **How to make a glove puppet**

STAR STEPS

1 Plan your writing. — *What will you need? How will you start?*

2 Remember, the order of the instructions has to be right. — *Use numbers to show the order of the instructions.*

3 Writing the instructions. — *Make sure you include all the information. Where? When? What? How?*

4 Vocabulary — *You can be quite bossy! Use commands like:*
Cut the string.
Draw two small eyes.
Try to be precise e.g. two <u>small</u> eyes.

5 Use illustrations and labels. — *They will help to make the instructions clearer.*

Star Tip
Illustrations really help people to follow instructions more easily!

Star Tip
Check your instructions are in the right order by trying them out.

WRITING NON-FICTION 27

Making a glove puppet

Help to finish the instructions by drawing the illustrations.

You will need:

pencil □   scissors □   fabric □   pins □

thread □   needle □   felt pens □   paper □

Now you need to get the instructions in the right order!

Order these muddled instructions by putting numbers in the boxes.

Then pin your template to the fabric. □

Next fold your fabric in half. □

Finally draw on a face. □

Cut out your template. □

First make a template. Draw around your hand on the piece of paper. [1]

Sew all around the edge of the puppet, sewing both pieces of fabric together. □

Cut around the template through both layers of fabric. □

Did you spot the clues we gave you? Words like *first*, *then*, and *next* help to get things in the right order!

Star Tip
Choose describing words carefully.

★ Take a thin piece of string.
★ Take a small piece of string.

Do they mean the same thing?

Star Tip
You need to be able to follow instructions for lots of things, such as:
★ for building a model
★ playing a game
★ recipes
★ operating a video

WRITING NON-FICTION

Writing a recount

It sounds complicated but it just means retelling something that's happened.

STAR STEPS

1 Plan your writing. — *Think about what you want to say.*

2 Make sure you cover question words. — *Who? Where? When? What? Why? How?*

3 Remember, the order of the events has to be right. — *Write things down in the order they happened. Use first, then, next, later, after, meanwhile, before.*

4 Middle — *Say why you think things happened.*

5 Ending — *Finish by saying how the event affected you.*

Star Tip
Try using exclamation marks to express surprise or excitement.
It was a terrible shock!
We were delighted!

Star Tip
Try using exciting descriptions for how things happened.
He cried. ✗
He began to sob. ✓

WRITING NON-FICTION

Practice questions

Improve this recount by adding in some words in the spaces.

Day out at the circus

On Wednesday our class went to the circus. We were so _____, everyone was smiling. As we _____ we bought candyfloss. Sally _____ dropped hers and began to sob_____. Just then a clown approached us. He gave Sally an _____ balloon. She stopped crying and we all cheered. Then a fantastic thing happened. He _____ each of us with a balloon. We cheered even louder than before. I think I liked my balloon as much as the show!

Use these words or think of others that would also fit.

presented, arrived, happy, immediately, enormous, loudly

Have a go at writing a recount here.

Try these titles, or use your own.

The day I got lost or When I broke my bike

Writing letters

Informal letters

It's great fun to get a letter, and one way to make sure you get one is to *send* one. So you had better start practising.

STAR STEPS

Question: How do I make a letter to a friend seem friendly and informal?

1 Plan your writing.
Think first. Always plan what you want to say.

2 Beginning
Always write your address at the top. Start your letter with **Hello** *or* **Hi** *or* **Dear**.

3 Vocabulary
You can write just as you would talk. It is OK to use shortened words, like don't, couldn't, it's, I'll.

4 Ending
Choose a friendly way to sign off. Bye for now, See you soon, Lots of love

Practice question

Write a letter to a friend.
Here are some things you could tell them about.

★ A football game you played in/went to
★ Your new pet
★ Your latest hobby

Star Tip
Don't forget you still need to use proper sentences. Keep checking for full stops and capital letters.

Star Tip
Try to write letters regularly to family and friends. You can send postcards too!

Formal letters

Remember, when you write to someone you don't know, you need to write a formal letter. Formal letters sound a bit posh, but have a go!

Question: How do I write a formal letter?

1 Plan your writing.
Think first. Always plan what you want to say.

2 Beginning
Always write your address at the top. Start your letter with Dear Mr, Dear Mrs or Dear Miss.

3 Vocabulary
You cannot write as you might talk. Use full words like this:
could not, would not, we are, you are

4 Ending
Use a formal way to sign off.
Yours sincerely,
Mr J. Bloggs
(include your surname)

Now look at these letters. Which one is formal and which is informal?

9 Lee Rd,
London

Dear Gem,
I'm so excited about your visit, I just can't wait. Mum says if the weather's OK she'll take us to the beach, so don't forget your swimming costume.
See you on Sunday,
Love,
Laura

3 Bridge Road,
Lewisham

Dear Mr Jones,
I would like to draw your attention to the state of Bridge Road Park. The park has a grassed area, which is well used. However, the children's play area is not used as it contains broken and dangerous equipment. Could you please let me know if there are plans to improve the park in the near future?
Yours sincerely,
Mrs V. Smith

Practice question

Have a go at writing a formal letter yourself and try to sound really posh!

Information writing

To begin with you need to research your topic. Read up on the subject you are interested in before you start to write.

Let's have a go at some information writing.

Topic: Dinosaurs

STAR STEPS

1 Plan your writing.
How do we know about dinosaurs?
What did they look like?
What did they eat?

2 Beginning
Remember to introduce your topic.
Dinosaurs are…

3 Writing about the topic.
Make sure you cover
Who? Where? When? What? Why? How?

4 Vocabulary
Use words that go with what you are writing about.
skeletons, prehistoric, fossils, plates, spines, meat-eater, plant-eater

5 Use illustrations and labels.
They will help to make the information clearer.

Star Tip
Don't forget you still need to use proper sentences. Keep checking for full stops and capital letters.

Star Tip
You can use describing words but don't turn it into a story!
T Rex was a vicious man-eater. ✓
T Rex liked playing fun games with his friend. ✗

WRITING NON-FICTION 33

Have a go at writing information about dinosaurs here.
Try to use the suggested words.

How do we know about dinosaurs?
_____
_____
_____

Draw your illustration here.

Some useful words
archaeologist, discovered, fossil, bones, buried, huge, reptiles, prehistoric

What did dinosaurs look like?
_____
_____
_____

Draw your illustration here.

Some useful words
Triceratops, horns, armour, tough, skull, neck shield, beak, heavy, enormous, Dimetrodon, spiny tail, short-legged, T Rex, long hind legs, meat-eater, sharp teeth, huge jaws, extremely small claws

What did they eat?
_____
_____
_____

Draw your illustration here.

Some useful words
plant-eaters, herbivores, leaves, bushes and trees, grasses, tough skin, armour, tails with spikes, meat-eaters, sharp tearing teeth, claws, fighting, defending, hunters

Punctuation

Remember full stops, capital letters and question marks are really important, so here's some practice!

Practise writing capital letters.
Fill in the gaps.

A B _ D E F _ H _ J _ L M
N O _ Q R _ T _ V W X _ Z

Practice questions

Put full stops, capital letters and question marks in the right places in these sentences.

1 everyone cheered as I crossed the finish line

2 we waited for the wizard to arrive

3 they were surrounded by treasure

4 how would we ever get out

5 she thought manchester was too far away

6 had the robbers seen me

7 jack ran as fast as he could

8 could this machine really work

9 the party was over and beth went home

10 i wish i could play for liverpool

Star Tip

Don't get confused! Capital letters are sometimes called upper case letters.

Guess what small letters are called. That's right – lower case letters!

Exclamation marks

An exclamation mark can take the place of a full stop. We use them to show excitement in our writing.

We can use exclamation marks when we are:

★ angry — *How dare you!*

★ surprised — *What a wonderful gift!*

★ happy — *I'm so pleased to see you!*

★ disgusted — *Oh that smell!*

★ shouting — *Get out of here!*

Practice questions

Work out which of these sentences need exclamation marks and add them in.

1 We walked to the shops
2 Wow, what a fantastic day
3 I never, ever wanted to see them again
4 Where do you live
5 Cheese on toast for lunch, again
6 My brother's name is Jack
7 I hate swimming

Try writing some phrases that need exclamation marks yourself.

_____
_____
_____
_____

Star Tip
Remember, don't use exclamation marks all the time – just when the writing is really exciting.

Star Tip
If you aren't sure what punctuation to use, read out the sentence to yourself. That may help you.

Using conjunctions

You can make your writing more interesting by using **conjunctions** to join shorter sentences together.

Question: How can you improve these sentences?

STAR STEPS

I was upset. Megan and Bella had eaten my sweets.

1 Read the question then read it again. — *Read the sentences carefully.*

2 Read the sentences aloud. — *This helps you hear ideas.*

3 Think of conjunctions you could use. — **if, so, because, when, until, after, while, before**

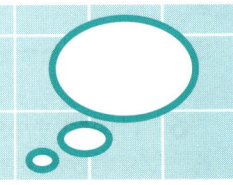

4 Choose a word that links the sentences. — I was upset so Megan and Bella had eaten my sweets. ✗

5 Does your sentence make sense? If not, choose another conjunction. — I was upset because Megan and Bella had eaten my sweets. ✓

Star Tip

To get used to conjunctions, write as many as you can think of here.

Practice questions

Change these short sentences by adding one of these conjunctions.

so   though   before   after   until

1 Joseph was bored. He went to the cricket match.
   _____

2 Bethany didn't like many vegetables. She sometimes ate broccoli.
   _____

3 Edward played in the garden. He ate his supper.
   _____

4 The match had finished. We went home.
   _____

5 I went to my class. The bell had gone.
   _____

6 There was nothing to watch on TV. We turned it off.
   _____

7 Clare did her homework. She went to bed.
   _____

8 It was too dark to see. Mum turned off the light.
   _____

Star Tip

Try not to use **and** or **then** too much in your writing. Don't do it like this!
*I saw a dog **and** it was brown **and** it was running **and** then it was barking **then** it stopped **then** a man came **then** he called the dog **then** the dog came.*

VOCABULARY

Using time connectives

Using time connectives helps you to make your writing easier to understand. Time connectives help to put the story in order. **First, afterwards, next, suddenly, at that moment** are all time connectives.

Question: How can you make these sentences make more sense?

STAR STEPS

Isobel was walking to the shops. Harry jumped out and scared her.

1 Read the question then read it again. — *Read the sentences carefully.*

2 Read the sentences aloud. — *This helps you hear ideas.*

3 Think of time connectives you could use. — then, afterwards, first, next, suddenly, before

4 Choose a word that describes *how* Ramon walked. — Isobel was walking to the shops at that moment Harry jumped out and scared her.

5 Does your sentence make sense? If not, choose another adverb. — Isobel was walking to the shops when suddenly Harry jumped out and scared her.

Star Tip
Write as many time connectives as you can think of here.

_____ _____ _____

_____ _____ _____

_____ _____ _____

Practice questions 1

Circle the time connectives in these sentences.

1 Hannah finished her football match then went home for supper.

2 After travelling all day, the brothers rested at home.

3 First we must see the monkeys, then we can go to the zebras.

4 One morning the snowman was there, then it disappeared.

Practice questions 2

Change these sentences by adding one of these connectives.

first   then   next   afterwards   suddenly

1 Charlie played with his cars. He played in the garden.
   _____

2 Joanne was walking towards the gate. Her brother, Andrew, shouted from the front door.
   _____

3 I am going to the shops. I will go to the cinema.
   _____

4 Sara did her homework. She played with her hamster.
   _____

Star Tip

Try not to use **then** all the time. It can make your writing a bit boring.

DON'T do it like this: *I went to school then I went to Robbie's house, then I had supper, then I went into the magic cupboard, then I found the treasure, then I came home.*

Vocabulary choices

Having good vocabulary means being able to use lots of different words and using them properly.

1 Never say **nice!**

Try some of these:
wonderful	great	sweet	kind	handsome	beautiful
considerate	generous	tasty	delicious	refreshing	

2 Think of different words for **said**.

whispered	called	cried	yelled	asked
whimpered	bellowed	screeched	laughed	shouted
questioned	replied	pleaded		

3 Think of words for **feelings**.

happy	delighted	glad	content	pleased	joyous
sad	miserable	sorrowful	wretched	gloomy	
scared	frightened	terrified	alarmed	shocked	

Star Tip
Notice new words in your reading books or comics and write them down.
Listen to words people use when they speak.

Star Tip
You will find lots of new words in a thesaurus. See if you can find one at school or in a library.

VOCABULARY 41

Practice questions

Can you think of some different words to put into these sentences?

The school disco

Here I was again, <u>fed up</u> and lonely. I hated the school disco but Mum had <u>forced</u> us to go, she helped organise it. "Let me stay at home, please," I <u>said</u>. "No way!" she <u>said</u>. I was <u>really mad</u>.

Now re-write this passage adding in more interesting vocabulary!

Here I was again…

_____
_____
_____
_____
_____
_____

Use a thesaurus or dictionary to help you add words to these word lists.

big _____

walked _____

cried _____

old _____

hot _____

cold _____

The Key Stage 1 Tests

What are SATs?

The Key Stage 1 National Tests, or SATs as they are commonly known, are assessments that take place at the end of Year 2. There are tests in Reading, Writing and Maths and these are supported by Teacher Assessment in all three areas.

The tests are usually carried out during May and are spread out over several weeks to ease the pressure on the children. They take place as part of a normal day and most schools do not tell the children they are doing a 'test'. The children will have done plenty of practices and preparation in school and the tests are usually carried out in the classroom with the teacher.

What do the levels mean?

The National Curriculum sets down levels children are expected to reach by certain ages. On average children will be at

- Level 2 by the end of Key Stage 1 (age 7)
- Level 4 by the end of Key Stage 2 (age 11)
- Level 5/6 at the end of Key Stage 3 (age 14)

Within each level there are strands A, B and C where A indicates the child is working confidently within the level, B is average and C shows they are just achieving within the level.

What do the tests consist of?

Writing

There are two Writing Tasks, a Spelling Test and a Handwriting Task. The Writing Tasks consist of a longer task, which is usually in the form of a story, and a shorter task, which will take a different form, perhaps a letter or a set of instructions. The children will be expected to work independently and spell and punctuate their work as best they can. The tasks are not timed but it is expected that the longer task should take about 45 minutes and the shorter one about 30 minutes.

There is also a separate Spelling Test where children are required to write a list of words read out by the teacher. There are about 20 words and the majority of them will be words the children have already come across.

Handwriting is also looked at. In some cases handwriting is assessed as part of the Writing Tasks. Children might be asked to copy out a part of their story in their best handwriting and will be expected to join some letters.

Reading

The Reading Test consists of a reading task and a separate comprehension test. During the reading task the child will read part of a book to a teacher and should be able to discuss the book and answer questions. Their ability to work out unknown words, read with good pace and expression and show an understanding of the story are all assessed.

For the reading comprehension test the children are given a reading booklet with a story and piece of non-fiction writing in. The children will be expected to read as much as they can independently and answer the questions that are in the booklet.

Maths

All children will take a written Maths Test. It covers most aspects of Number and Shape, Space and Measuring. There are also some mental maths questions that the teacher will read out. There is an emphasis on Using and Applying mathematical knowledge and children are often asked to solve simple problems and explain their answers.

What is the Teacher Assessment?

At the end of Key Stage 1 teachers also carry out their own assessments of each child in the areas of Reading, Writing and Maths. These assessments are based on classroom observations and looking at a child's work over a period of time. Usually the Teacher Assessment level is the same as the SATs level but occasionally there are discrepancies. It is worth remembering that the SATs level is an indication of how your child performed on one particular day under test-like conditions and only covers small areas of the curriculum. The Teacher Assessment gives a more rounded view of the child's ability and covers all aspects of the English and Maths curriculums.

Helping your child do well

There is no right way to prepare your child and it is not necessary to spend hours revising for a test. Most children do not even know they are doing a test and this is the best preparation for them!

Most schools do not tell the children they are taking a test as this adds a huge amount of pressure on them to get it all right. They will have had opportunities to try practice papers, doing as much as they can independently. When the real test comes it is usually seen as just another classroom activity.

Working at home with your child

Working through these books with your child will help reinforce what they have learnt during Year 2 and get them used to answering test type questions. Here are some things you can do:

- Find time when you are both relaxed and happy.
- Choose a quiet spot without distractions.
- Keep sessions short, especially when you see your child is getting bored or frustrated.
- Work through examples in this book together and then allow your child to have a go at the practice questions. Read the *Star Tips* together – you could ask your child to come up with different voices for the characters!
- Encourage them if they find something difficult. Try not to let your frustrations show, as they will pick up on this and become more anxious themselves. Take a short break and try again tomorrow.
- Try to make all activities meaningful for them. When practising writing letters, why not write one to a friend or relative? This will encourage them to practise their reading when they get a reply! Or ask them to write out your shopping list for you. Let them play with your money and encourage them to work out totals and calculate change using real coins.

All children will find questions on the papers that they cannot do or find very challenging and some can find this hard to cope with. You can help by encouraging them to have a go at something difficult and not to give up when it gets tough. A challenging jigsaw puzzle is a good place to start.

Of course, preparation does not always have to take the form of pencil and paper work. Children learn by doing so try some fun practical activities:

- Read to your child. This will help greatly with their writing as they learn about story structure and acquire new vocabulary.
- Ask your child to tell you a bedtime story for a change.
- Play games. Board games such as snakes and ladders or dominoes are great for all those number skills. Use long car journeys for word games.
- Play shops with REAL money!

Often children's concerns or worries about the tests come from parents' own concerns about their child. Unless your child's school tells the children they are doing a test, try not to talk to them, or in front of them, about the tests. Keep things as normal as possible during the test period and take opportunities to celebrate their success. A word of praise from a parent goes a long way!

Good luck and have fun!

Answers

Page 6
1) Gemma put her hat on.
2) Robert went into the shop.
3) The brown dog was barking.
4) Cats like to sleep in the sun.

Page 7
Tenses
1) I was riding
2) I will sing
3) We write

Mistakes
1) She **wrote** her letter yesterday.
2) I will **play** at school today.
3) Marie **swam** ten lengths of the pool.
4) Jack will **drive** to school tomorrow.

Page 8
Answers will vary but children should choose adjectives that are appropriate, for example, **fierce tiger**.

Page 9
Answers will vary but children should choose adverbs that are appropriate, for example, **ran quickly**.

Page 10
Make sure that children keep within the lines and the letter formations are legible. This can be substituted with work from the school's own handwriting programme.

Page 11
Syllables
Joshua   3
Keith   1
Robert   2
Una   2
Bethany   3
Francis   2
Rebecca   3
Laura   2
Kevin   2

Page 12
Speech Marks
1) "Well done to you all," said Mrs Cranky.
2) "Try throwing underarm Jack," advised his mum.
3) "I don't care!" yelled the strange girl.
4) "Please take us to the pictures," we begged.
5) Mum called up the stairs to us, "Have you tidied your room?"
6) "Do you know the park is closed?" asked the park keeper.
7) Tom shouted again, "I'm not going with you!"
8) "Your project must be finished by tomorrow!" the teacher bellowed.
9) "Why do you have to be so noisy?" moaned Gran.
10) "I hope you like it," Dad beamed.

Page 13
Speech Marks
2) "Wash the dishes!" ordered Mum.
3) "Come and see the flowers," called Annie.
4) "I live on a farm," replied Josh.
5) "Watch out!" we shouted to the others.
6) "I slipped in the mud," laughed Frank.
7) "I have lost my ball," sighed Jack.
8) "Please take us to the park, Auntie Suzy," we pleaded.
Answers will vary but children should choose words that are appropriate substitutes for 'said', for example, "Watch out!" we shouted to the others.

Page 15
Use another piece of paper to cover up these words so that children can practise their spellings. Children can check their answers themselves.

Page 16
Use another piece of paper to cover up these words so that children can practise their spellings. Children can check their answers themselves.

ANSWERS

Page 19
1) The rain poured through the roof.
2) Most cats like milk.
3) Fireworks exploded in the night sky.
4) You can find lots of shells on the seashore.

Subject	Verb and ending
The young boy	wished he could become like his older brother.
A magic slipper	was on the princess's foot.
My favourite toy	is the bike I got for my birthday.
The startled horse	bolted.
Leo's football boots	hurt his feet.
The puppy's tail	wagged excitedly.
The raging hurricane	destroyed everything in its path.
A relaxing holiday	is always welcome.

Page 22
Answers will vary.

Page 23
Look at the suggestions on pages 20-21 and make sure children have followed the planning process.

Page 25
Answers will vary.

Page 27
Instructions should go in this order:

First make a template. Draw around your hand on the piece of paper.	1
Cut out your template.	2
Next fold your fabric in half.	3
Then pin your template to the fabric.	4
Cut around the template through both layers of fabric.	5
Sew all around the edge of the puppet, sewing both pieces of fabric together.	6
Finally draw on a face.	7

Page 29
Answers will vary. Children could try to add in the correct words from the list at the bottom and then go on to suggest alternatives.

Page 30
Answers will vary.

Page 31
The letter on the right hand side of the page is more formal.
Children should follow the flow chart to write their own letter.

Page 33
Answers will vary.

ANSWERS

Page 34
ABCDEFGHIJKLMOPQRSTUVWXYZ

1) Everyone cheered as I crossed the finish line.
2) We waited for the wizard to arrive.
3) They were surrounded by treasure.
4) How would we ever get out?
5) She thought Manchester was too far away.
6) Had the robbers seen me?
7) Jack ran as fast as he could.
8) Could this machine really work?
9) The party was over and Beth went home.
10) I wish I could play for Liverpool.

Page 35
Exclamation marks should go on sentences 2, 3 and 7.

Page 37
1) until
2) though
3) after or before
4) so
5) before or after
6) so
7) until or before
8) after

Page 39
Practice Questions 1
1) then
2) After
3) First, then
4) One morning

Practice Questions 2
Answers will vary but children should choose time connectives that are appropriate, for example: **First Charlie played with his cars, then he played in the garden.**

Page 41
Some word choices below:

Big	large	huge	enormous	vast
Walked	strolled	ambled	marched	hiked
Cried	wailed	moaned	whined	sobbed
Old	ancient	aged	elderly	getting-on
Hot	warm	boiling	scorching	sizzling
Cold	freezing	icy	frosty	bitter